*Saint Paul tells us to "pray without ceasing" (1 Thess 5:17).
Diana Macalintal responds to that happy admonition in her
poetic* The Work of Your Hands. *Whether you are looking for
a prayer for procrastinators on the feast of Saint Expeditus or a
prayer when Mass feels empty, a blessing for those in love or
a blessing for graduates, Macalintal will help you lift your minds
and hearts to our gracious God. And graced prayers and
blessings these are.*

> Bishop Robert Morneau
> Pastor of Resurrection Parish
> Auxiliary Bishop Emeritus of the
> Diocese of Green Bay

*Diana Macalintal offers us a creative and inspiring source rich
in possibilities.* The Work of Your Hands—*a collection of prayers
and blessings, touching the ordinary and extraordinary rhythms
of human life—is sure to enrich our spiritual journey. Savor an
outstanding and fresh resource for everyday reflection, for special
celebrations and particular needs.*

> Edith Prendergast, RSC
> Director of Religious Education
> Archdiocese of Los Angeles

*I read a lot of books and manuscripts, but this one caught me by
surprise. I could not read it in one sitting. I kept it near me and
took up one prayer after another, slowly letting them sink in.
This is a book I will keep on my nightstand for many years, a book
I will never put away. From the tender words in the introduction
to the final "Amen!" it's fantastic. It comes from the heart of
Diana Macalintal whose passion creeps into every line. But make
no mistake: it's beautiful but it's also disturbing. Certain lines of
these prayers will not fade away from your heart easily; they will
linger until God has touched you through them with his power.*

> Bill Huebsch
> Director of the ThePastoralCenter.com
> Author of The Art of Self-giving Love

Fresh, evocative language from the hands of one steeped in the richness of the scriptures and attentive to the deep longings of the human heart. Diana Macalintal has graced us with a gift—prayers for every season of life worth placing on our lips and planting in our hearts over a lifetime. This collection gives voice to the depths of our joy, pain, and everything in between, helping us to see God's quiet and constant presence amidst it all.

Tony Alonso, composer and author

Diana Macalintal is that rare and gifted artist who has the ability to describe the indescribable. She is the poet who comes along only once in a great, long while with the capacity to image the unimaginable, opening our senses to the profound in our everyday midst whether it might be Christ in the least fortunate reaching out to bless us or the wisdom figure of her own grandmother who loves and nurtures God's creation into being giving us the gift of Diana. This collection of prayers is the promise of a personal retreat, a moment away from the noise of our daily lives. All great artists summon us beyond ourselves, and after spending time in this collection of prayers, you will emerge from this book's pages a different person than when you first opened them. Someone will be fed or held in your care for your having spent time in the world Diana opens to us.

John K. Flaherty
Liturgy Committee Chair & Music Director,
Los Angeles Religious Education Congress
Associate Director of Campus Ministry,
Loyola Marymount University

Ever feel tongue-tied in prayer? Ever wonder what you could say to God, and how you could say it? Let Diana Macalintal help you with this new book of her poetic prayers and her prayerful poems. They are both beautiful prayers themselves and beautiful invitations to deeper meditation and richer contemplation.

James Martin, SJ
Author of *Jesus: A Pilgrimage*

The Work of Your Hands

The Work of Your Hands

Prayers for Ordinary
and Extraordinary
Moments of Grace

Diana Macalintal

LITURGICAL PRESS

Collegeville, Minnesota

www.litpress.org

Design by Ann Blattner.

Cover photos: Mural in the apse of the old church, now the Great Hall, at Saint John's University. Modeled on the *Christus Pantocrator*, Christ the Almighty. Beuronese art by Clement Frischauf, 1939. Photos courtesy of the monks of Saint John's Abbey, Collegeville, Minnesota. Used with permission.

Cross: Illustration by Br. Frank Kacmarcik, OblSB, Saint John's Abbey, Collegeville, Minnesota. Used with permission.

Photo on page 10 by Lesley Mendoza.

3   4   5   6   7   8   9

Library of Congress Cataloging-in-Publication Data

Macalintal, Diana.
    The work of your hands : prayers for ordinary and extraordinary moments of grace / Diana Macalintal.
      pages   cm
     ISBN 978-0-8146-3803-3 — ISBN 978-0-8146-3828-6 (ebook)
    1. Prayers.   I. Title.

BV260.M155   2014
242'.8—dc23

2013041021

Fruit   12

Prayers

Prayer for the Work of Our Hands   17

Prayer for Procrastinators on the Feast of
Saint Expeditus   18

Prayer to Accept Change   20

Prayer for Dreamers   22

Prayer for the Care of the Earth   24

Thanksgiving upon Receiving Good News   25

Prayer for Good Speech   26

Prayer for the Next Time I Meet Christ   28

Prayer When Lighting Candles   30

Prayer When Mass Feels Empty 31

Parent's Prayer for Sunday Morning 32

Child's Prayer Before Trick-or-Treating 33

Prayer Before Preparing a Family Feast 34

Prayer for the New Year 35

Prayer for Keeping Resolutions 36

Valentine's Prayer When Your Heart Is Broken 37

Prayer When Money Is Tight 38

Prayer When You Have Nothing Left to Give 39

Traveler's Prayer 40

Prayer Before Confession After a Long Absence 41

Prayer in Time of Violence 42

Prayer When Living with Cancer 44

Prayer at an Unexpected Pregnancy 46

Godparent's Prayer 48

Parent's Prayer When Children Are Leaving Home 49

Child's Prayer for Grandparents 50

Prayer Before Family Reunions 51

Prayer with the Woman at the Well 52

Blessings

Blessing of Those Who Are Sick   56

Blessing of Families in Their Homes   57

Meal Prayer of Gratitude for Those Who Feed Us   58

Blessing of Brains   59

Blessing of Students in Faith Formation   60

Blessing of a Classroom   61

Blessing of Graduates   62

Blessing of a Soldier Home from War   64

Blessing for Those in Love   66

Blessing of Christmas Cards Before Mailing   67

Blessing of Calendars on the Feast of the Epiphany   68

Epiphany Home Blessing   70

Lenten Meal Blessing   71

Blessing of Animals   72

Saying Goodbye to a Dying Pet   74

Blessing for All Creation   76

My grandmother taught me to pray, though she spoke no prayer out loud. We lived together, three generations under the same roof. In our yard, I watched her build trellises, loosen dirt, and dig neatly spaced rows along the garage. Her hands transformed that dog run of brown nothingness into a green maze of curlicues, vines, and beans. Next to them were the eggplants as big as your head. Across the yard were the roses, pink and huge with thorns that cut deep.

In the same way, my grandmother shaped a barren corner of her bedroom into a shrine of icons, rosaries, palms, candles, and holy cards. Roses guarded the college photo of the child she lost to cancer and the wedding portrait with the husband she would lose years later. (Soon after, another child would complete that trinity.) She sat there each night, praying but making no sound.

My life's vocation has been to help people pray the liturgy, with all the words, music, and artistry I could muster. But my grandmother's vocation has been to make her very life a prayer, to cultivate everything around her, thorns and all, into a garden of praise to God.

Like gardening and liturgy, prayer is work, our work and God's, the fruit of which we may never see. But it is there, hidden and waiting to flourish. I dedicate this book to my grandmother, Irene, for it is the fruit of the vine she planted in me long ago.

Diana Macalintal

Fruit

Even when I was young, my grandmother's hands
     were old
Aged with cracked crevices, twisted knots for knuckles
She tilled the soil of our garden with mud-blackened
     fingers and
Dirt-stained nails until there was space for seed

Dig, plant, water, watch—a small thing done by a
     small woman
With small arthritic hands, but how grand a garden
     she grew
Beans, eggplants, lemons, oranges, squash in the fall,
     strawberries in summer
And roses enough for her only son's grave

Her hands taught me to cling not to fear but to faith
Not to grab for what seems safe but to reach for the
     one in danger
Not to clutch to our own comfort but to hold firm the
     hand of another

Could it be that God's hands are just like hers, dug deep
    in the soil
Of our hearts, fearless of muck, patient in want,
    searching
Searching for the stream of light welling up beneath
    the mud
Mud our Savior smeared on blinded eyes
Eyes that witnessed death come back to life
Life that does tender small things
With immensely great and aching love

Let us be like God's hands
Holding firm to the beauty within
Grafted to the one true Vine
For on that Tree all fear has ended
A tree bloodied by Life itself
Watered by Grace eternal
Laden with Love unbounded
Free for the taking and
Sweet on the lips

Prayers

Yet, LORD, you are our father;
we are the clay and you our potter:
we are all the work of your hand.

—Isaiah 64:7

Prayer for the Work of Our Hands

Blessed are you, Lord God,
Creator of all that is good,
for in your mercy you give us work
that we may be cocreators with you.

With hands to fashion and form,
minds to imagine what has yet to be,
hearts to care for what we have made,
and a spirit to impart to our own creations,
we rejoice in the labor you give us.

By imitating you, our God and Maker,
we continue to shape the world,
to name it and claim it
and be good stewards of your good gifts
through the life-giving Spirit that renews the earth.

Keep us mindful of the power you share with us
that we may create only that which leads to peace.
May the work of our hands and our visions and dreams
collaborate with your good will,
which continues to build for us your kingdom on earth.
We ask this through Christ our Lord.
Amen.

Prayer for Procrastinators on the Feast of Saint Expeditus

Saint Expeditus, perhaps a fictional saint, is the patron saint of procrastinators. His feast day is celebrated on April 19 (four days after tax day) or, as his followers like to say, whenever you get around to it. Traditional images of him feature the words hodie *and* cras, *Latin for* today *and* tomorrow.

'Ve done it again, Lord.
I've missed another deadline.
Why can't I ever be on time?

Imagine if Noah had pulled an all-nighter
or the Magi had put off making travel plans—
I guess if salvation had depended on me,
your will would never be done!

But you also chose the less punctual to show your glory:
Jonah, the ultimate procrastinator,
and the infamous stragglers who wound up first.

Yet, Lord, I know that *now* is the time
and *today* is the day of salvation.
So help me do what needs to be done—
today and not tomorrow.

Keep me focused on the path—
looking ahead and not behind.

With the help of Saint Expeditus
and all who patiently wait for me,
teach me to order the chaos of my day,
that each moment may be spent wisely
in timely service to you.
Amen.

Prayer to Accept Change

Just when I thought I had it all figured out, Lord,
things change again.
When will I be able to rest
in the comfort of knowing what comes next?

You, who transcend all time,
who created the stars and set them in place,
you, who are ageless yet known in every age,
grant me the grace to accept
the changes that are happening.

Empty my heart of anxiety,
and fill it instead with wonder and awe.
Release me from the chains of complacency,
and bind me to your ever-moving Spirit.

When the things I believed to be permanent and stable
are left by the wayside,
enfold me in your undying love
that I may remember in whom all things are bound.

When fear of something new paralyzes me,
and grief cripples me with anger
over the loss of what had been,
send your angels to give me a gentle push
over that frightening edge into the unknown,
so that I may learn to trust in you.

For you alone are eternal.
You alone are enduring.
You alone are the everlasting Lord.
And in you alone will this restless world find peace.
Amen.

Prayer for Dreamers

God of our waking and our sleeping,
in every age,
you have spoken to your prophets
in dreams and visions
and have promised that
our sons and daughters shall prophesy
through your Spirit.

Through the dreams of young Joseph,
you saved your people from famine.
In the visions of King Solomon,
you blessed your land with wisdom.
Because of dreams,
elder Joseph acted quickly
to protect your only Son from harm.

And through the revelation announced to Mary,
you brought forth a new King and a new dream
for all the world.

Bless those who continue to seek you in dreams.
Open their ears to hear you in their visions,
loosen their tongues to speak your word,
strengthen their hands to respond swiftly in action,
and embolden their hearts that what they hear in the dark
they may proclaim in the light.

Make us all dreamers who tirelessly pursue
the vision of your Kingdom.
We ask this through Christ our Lord.
Amen.

Prayer for the Care of the Earth

God our Father and Creator, we give you thanks
for the wonder of creation which inspires us,
the fruit of the Earth which feeds us,
the beauty of nature which grounds us,
and the joy of life which gives us hope.
Heal the places where your creation has been marred,
and restore all creatures to the splendor of your glory,
that all may delight once again in your goodness.
We ask this through Christ our Lord.
Amen.

Thanksgiving upon Receiving Good News

Blessed are you, Lord God, who bring us good news!
When the years had worn on, barren and joyless,
you came to our door as angels in disguise,
blessing our home with new life and laughter.

When all seemed dark and despair overshadowed us,
you met us on the road as an unexpected stranger,
opening our eyes and hearts to the fire of your love.

And as we wept at the mouth of the tomb in a
        springtime garden,
you spoke our name, concealed as a common field hand,
sending us out to proclaim, "We have seen the Lord!"

We praise you and we bless you
for the good news you bring us this day.
Make us bearers of your life-giving message
that fills our world with wonder, hope, and surprise.
Amen.

Prayer for Good Speech

Gracious God, with only words
you created the universe and called it "good."
Help me, then, to use my words well,
to create only life and give blessing this day.

You numbered the stars and called each one by name.
Let me cherish each person I meet
and speak their name with reverence.

You promised that your word is very near to us,
already in our mouths and in our hearts.
Give me your Spirit, and teach me what to say.
Stand guard over my mouth and temper my heart
when emotions race and words so easily cut.
Help me know when to speak up,
to be a cry for the poor and a voice in the desert,
and teach me the wisdom to know when to be silent.

Your words calmed the seas, raised the dead,
forgave the sinner, and comforted the mourning.
Give me the grace to speak the simple words:
"Please" and "Thank you." "Yes." "I love you."

And strengthen me to say the words that need to be said:
"I was wrong." "I'm sorry." "Forgive me." "I forgive you."
Let my "yes" be "yes," my "no" mean "no,"
and my promises be kept.

Above all, may I remember that
even if I speak with the tongues of angels,
yet do not have love, I am simply making noise.
So let my tongue be silenced if ever I forget you.

Lord, today, make me your word and open my lips, (✠)*
and my mouth shall proclaim your praise.

Make the Sign of the Cross on your lips.

Prayer for the Next Time I Meet Christ

I see them, Lord, every morning,
standing on the same street corner.
They hold their tattered signs—
"will work for food"—
with every bit of dignity they have.
As I drive by, they raise their hand
in blessing.

I walk by them on my lunch break,
leaning up against a wall,
their few possessions tucked close by.
A dirty hand reaches out
in a sign of peace.
"Spare some change?" they ask,
as I avoid eye contact.
"God bless you" is their answer
to my silence.

Lord, when did we see you hungry or thirsty,
a stranger and alone?
When did we see you at all?

Forgive me, God, for what I have done
and for what I have failed to do.
And I ask blessed Mary, ever virgin,
all the angels and saints,
and you, my brothers and sisters
whom I have passed by,
to pray for me,
that next time,
I will stop to meet Christ.

Prayer When Lighting Candles

Christ, be our light
when darkness draws near.
May we be your light
for all those in fear.
Let the light we received
from godparents' hands
shine brightly and strong
throughout all our lands.

Prayer When Mass Feels Empty

They say the Mass is the source and summit,
    but lately, Lord, it's just been empty.
Yet you have promised never to abandon us.
So do not let me grumble,
but make me instead an instrument of your peace.
Where there is apathy, let me be your passion.
Where there is coldness, let me be your warmth.
Where there is unwelcome, an open hand.
And where there's division, communion.
O Master, grant that I may never seek
so much to be filled as to be emptied of myself,
to be right as to listen,
to be comforted as to be moved to action.
For it is in giving ourselves that we receive you,
in forgiving others that we are forgiven,
and in dying to what we require that we gain all we need.

Parent's Prayer for Sunday Morning

God, help us get to church today
with minimal fuss and fighting,
with everyone dressed and ready to pray,
with all our bags packed, prepared for anything.
And if the kids get fussy and distracted,
please let there be a song to soothe them,
a colorful window to enchant them,
and kind pew mates to accept our flaws.

Child's Prayer Before Trick-or-Treating

God, bless all the people we will meet.
Let our visit with them be a pleasant treat.
Whatever the costumes we wear tonight,
may we all be clothed with Christ's light.
Protect us from danger and the devil's ways,
that tomorrow with the saints we may sing your praise.

Prayer Before Preparing a Family Feast

Lord, you know all the things that still need to be done—
the cooking and cleaning,
the preparation and anticipation,
the anxiety and worry that everything will be just right.
As I prepare this meal, help me also to prepare myself
that I may not be distracted by all these concerns.
And when you enter this home and sit at this table,
may I sit beside you and remember that

> only one thing is needed:

to love you with all my heart, with all my being,
with all my strength, and with all my mind,
and to love my neighbor as myself.
Amen.

Prayer for the New Year

God of every time and season,
you give us another year to fill with new beginnings.
We have so many dreams for this year,
so many promises we want to keep,
so many new habits we want to learn.
Yet so much from last year is still left undone.

Erase our failings of the old year,
clear away the decay left by our complacency,
and wipe clean the slate of broken covenants
    from the year gone by.
As the calendar changes and the old gives way to the new,
help us not to dwell on the past
but to use its memory to move us ever forward
    to your kingdom.

Renew our hope and strengthen our resolve
so that we may serve you faithfully through every season
and walk joyfully each day of the year.
We ask this through Christ our Lord.
Amen.

Prayer for Keeping Resolutions

I made a promise I want to keep,
but I feel I'm straying like little lost sheep.
Lord, guide me and help me find my way back,
and give my resolve the strength I lack.

Valentine's Prayer When Your Heart Is Broken

It's February again, God,
and I'm surrounded by reminders
of my broken heart.

Like fancy cards and paper cutouts,
we give away our hearts so easily.
And too often in return,
we receive only broken promises.

But you, O Lord, are ever-faithful,
you who heal the brokenhearted
and bind up all our wounds.

Bind me now to your Son's Sacred Heart
that the ache I feel may draw me closer
to those whom he loved
even when they turned away.
Let my heart not become a heart of stone,
roughened by bitterness
or calloused by doubt,
but let it be a heart of flesh,
strengthened by your unbreakable promise,
willing to give,
ready to forgive,
and open to trying again.

Prayer When Money Is Tight

Gracious God,
you tell me to look at the birds in the air
who don't work or sow,
yet they are fed each day by your hand.
But Lord, they can fly where they need to go,
while I still need to put gas in the car.
And you say to look at the flowers in the field
who don't worry about what they will wear,
yet you clothe them in splendor and majesty.
But Lord, lilies might dress up my dinner table,
but they won't feed my hungry family.

Giver of all good gifts,
I know you can't give me wings to fly or a life free of worry.
So please give me instead a heart overflowing
    with trust in you.
Though I may not get all the things that I ask for,
I know you will give me everything that I need.
When money is tight and anxiety is near,
open my heart to give freely of myself
that I might be abundantly rich in you.
Amen.

Prayer When You Have Nothing Left to Give

Lord, I have nothing left to give.
I'm exhausted and worn out.
Yet so many still ask for more.
Grant me that last ounce of strength
that sustained you on the cross
and allowed you to give
one last word of forgiveness,
that I may be gentle
with others and with myself.
And when that too is spent,
help me stay present even in my emptiness,
and let my presence be
the first and last gift
I have to give.
Amen.

Traveler's Prayer

Bless me, Lord, as I begin this adventure.
Open my eyes to see you in the people I will meet.
Open my ears to hear your word in new
    and surprising ways.
Open my hands to be your blessing
    in whatever situation I find myself.
And open my heart to receive you wherever I may go.
Protect me from harm as I travel
and give your wisdom to those I rely on for my safety.
When my travel is ended and my journey complete,
bring me home again, renewed by your love.
Amen.

Prayer Before Confession After a Long Absence

I confess, Lord, it's been a while,
and I feel ashamed.
My guilt just seemed to get in the way,
and now I've put this off for too long.
Why do I let myself stay so far from you
when I know in my heart
that you have never left?
I am afraid, Lord, that if I reveal myself to you,
show you who I have become,
you will not recognize me as your own.
So I beg, look upon me
as you would look upon your Son, Jesus,
that you might see and love in me
what you see and love in Christ.
Then when I rise up and go to you,
I shall be overwhelmed with love
when I see you running to me
with your arms wide open.
Amen.

Prayer in Time of Violence

I have to admit, God,
that sometimes it's hard
to even call your name.

On days like this
I can't help but think
that if you had been there,
we wouldn't be here—

—here in a world where
so much violence
has changed everything

—here where such bloodshed
fills today's news
even as many more die
each day, unnoticed and alone.

But here is where we need you,
and here is where we cry to you.
Be here with us, Lord, be here.

Let us be angry for what has been done,
but don't let us be consumed by it
that we no longer recognize ourselves
as your creation.

Give peace to the children.
Unbind them from the bonds of grief and fear
that they may become again
children of joy, of love, of trust, and hope.

And not today, Lord, but in time,
if there's at all any room in our hearts to forgive,
then so let it be,
for we all need to be created again.

Be here with us, Lord, be here,
right where we are, as broken as we are.
Be here with us, Lord, be here.
Amen.

Prayer When Living with Cancer

Lord God, even before I was born,
you knit me together in my mother's womb.
Every cell of my body you know,
and every inch of my skin
you yourself shaped
onto my flesh and bones.
Not a single hair on my head goes uncounted,
and no tear of mine escapes your gaze.

So I know you can make me whole again.

From the depths of this disease,
I cry out to you, O God,
for I am convinced
that neither cancer, nor tumor,
nor chemo, nor radiation,
nor fear, nor doubt,
nor isolation, nor pain
will be able to separate me from your love
and the wonder of the person
you created me to be.

From my first breath, you made me holy.
Fashion me again with your Spirit,
and fill this sacred and broken body with new life,
that every breath to my last
may proclaim
your mighty and wondrous deeds.
Amen.

Prayer at an Unexpected Pregnancy

"In the sixth month, the angel Gabriel was sent from God
to a town of Galilee called Nazareth,
to a virgin betrothed to a man named Joseph,
of the house of David, and the virgin's name was Mary."

(Luke 1:26-27)

Dear Lord, how can this be?—
New life inside of me?
This wasn't in my plans,
and I have too many questions, too many doubts.

Why me? Why now? Will I be good enough?
Can I handle this? What if something bad happens?
Am I ready at all?

Calm my doubts, and ease my fears, Lord.
Help me believe that you are with me in every moment,
especially when I feel alone.
Let me not be afraid of the plans you have prepared for me
and to walk this new path with peace.

Bless this baby, your creation and my child.
Protect it from harm as it grows.
Bless too all who will help me along the way.
Give us enough love, patience,
hope, and joy to share with one another.

Holy Mary, Mother of God,
let me be brave like you
that I may respond to this invitation as you did—
filled with grace, blessed with favor,
and courageous enough to say,
"May it be done to me according to your word."
Amen.

Godparent's Prayer

Good and gracious God,
for some reason, you chose me
to be a companion to *N.* in our life of faith.
I don't have any special wisdom to give him/her.
But I can give him/her my love for you
and for Jesus' way of life.

Help me remember that it is always you
who will give me the words I need to say
at just the right time.
Help me trust that it is always you
who will be our guide when we are unsure of the way.
Bless me with stronger faith and love for you
that *N.* may grow to love you even more.
And bless too my own godparents
who stood by my side
and led me to your font and altar.

As we make our way to our heavenly home,
may all of us walk together each day
with faith, hope, and love, ever joyful in your Spirit.
We ask this through Christ our Lord.
Amen.

Parent's Prayer When Children Are Leaving Home

Gracious God,
you blessed me with the gift of this child
and entrusted me with his/her care.
Now he/she leaves this home
and begins a new life apart from me.
Surround him/her with good people,
and watch over him/her each day.
Let him/her know that I will always be near
whenever he/she may need me.
Heal any hurts we may harbor with one another,
and forgive our failings as we learn
to be in a new kind of relationship with each other.
And when the sight of his/her empty room
pierces my heart with sadness,
may I find comfort in knowing that my child
is your child too,
filled with your grace and sheltered by your love.
Amen.

Child's Prayer for Grandparents

Dear God, please bless my grandparents.
Thank you for the life they gave my parents
and for the life they give to me.

For the ways they helped me and made me strong,
    I give thanks.
For the ways they love me no matter what, I rejoice.
For the ways they have paved the road
that leads me here, I am grateful.

Let them grow in wisdom and joy in life.
Let them find peace and rest from their work.
Let them be healed of every sickness and pain.
And let them see with their own eyes
the glory of your Son, Jesus,
in the love of their children and grandchildren.

Bless them always until they come to rest in you.
We ask this through Christ our Lord.
Amen.

Prayer Before Family Reunions

God, I will be seeing my family soon,
and it has been so long since I have been with them.
I am a different person now, and I am sure they are too.
Yet I still feel the same hurts that never went away,
the same wounds that never healed,
the same grudges that were never settled,
and the same anxiety of falling into old habits.
Fill me, Lord, with your peace, forgive my faults
    as I forgive,
and help me love my family as I know you love them.
With the Holy Family as our companions,
bless our time together and strengthen the bonds
    between us
that we may grow more in love with each other
until we are perfectly united forever in your kingdom.
We ask this through Christ our Lord.
Amen.

Prayer with the Woman at the Well

We know her darkest secrets,
  yet we don't even know her name.
How often we go by hearsay
in deciding who gets our attention.

Help me, Lord, to see
beyond the boundaries,
beyond the labels,
beyond the empty bucket,
or lack thereof,
to the flood of grace that awaits
if only we stop to talk with the stranger.

Blessings

Blessing of Those Who Are Sick

Healer of our every ill,
you watch over us as a mother over her child
and care for us with a father's love.
Lift up your servant, *N.*, who places his/her trust in you.
Free him/her from this sickness,
and give back to him/her the joy of your salvation.
Give your power of healing to his/her doctors, caregivers,
and all who minister to his/her needs.
May our brother/sister and all who seek healing
be strengthened in their weakness
to unite with us again in the assembly of your people,
where we will give you praise and glory, for ever and ever.
Amen.

Blessing of Families in Their Homes

God, our Father, in your Son, Jesus,
we become one family.
Bless this family and our earthly home.
Unite us closer together and make us holy,
heal our hurts and forgive our failings,
and grant us joy each and every day of the year.
Fill this home with abundant love,
and let no one leave here empty of hope.
May this home shelter all who dwell here
until we are all sheltered safely in your arms.
We ask this through Christ our Lord.
Amen.

Meal Prayer of Gratitude for Those Who Feed Us

Leader: Blessed are you, Creator God, for providing
the rain that waters the earth:
  All: *Blessed be God for ever.*

Blessed are you, Creator God, for sending the sun that
warms the fields: *Blessed . . .*

Blessed are you, God of Work, for strengthening the
hands that harvest the crops: *Blessed . . .*

Blessed are you, God of Work, for guiding the way of
those who deliver the yield: *Blessed . . .*

Blessed are you, Giver of Life, for inspiring the cooks
with imagination and love: *Blessed . . .*

Blessed are you, Giver of Life, for feeding us with the
love of family and friends: *Blessed . . .*

We give you thanks, loving God, for all these good gifts
and bless you for the food we are about to receive.
Let the sharing of our lives and the feasting at this table
be a foretaste of the joy of your heavenly banquet.
We ask this through Christ our Lord.
Amen.

Blessing of Brains

God, Creator of all things and of human intellect,
bless these students with orderly thinking,
curiosity for the work of your creation,
and a creative spirit in their studies.

Lord Jesus, Son of God, help them remain focused.
Give them eyes to see the connections between their study
and its value for life and service to others.
Energize them and get their brains working.
Send your Holy Spirit upon them
to give them flexibility of thought and expression,
good memory and calm nerves,
the ability to organize their thinking
and comprehend theories and facts
that they may express them with clarity and flair.
May your Spirit help them
to overcome any discouragement
and to rejoice in their accomplishment.

God our Wisdom, in whom we live, move,
         and have our being,
bless your sons and daughters.
Bless their brains and every part of their lives.
We ask this through Christ our Lord.
Amen.

Blessing of Students in Faith Formation

Eternal God, your wisdom is beyond our
    understanding,
yet it is revealed to us in the life and love of Jesus,
    your Son.
Bless these daughters and sons of yours
who have answered your call to grow in faith.
Enlighten them with your Word
    and fill them with your Spirit
that they may follow the path that leads to your wisdom.
Open their eyes that they may see your presence each day,
open their ears that they may hear your voice
    in unexpected places,
open their minds that they may understand
    the mystery of your love,
and open their hearts that they may be
    joyful companions with us
as we continue to grow in likeness to the mind of Christ.
Grant this through Christ our Lord.
Amen.

Blessing of a Classroom

God, our Teacher and Guide,
your wisdom is greater
than our minds can comprehend,
yet you give us the ability to learn and seek truth.

We give you thanks for this classroom
for forming our youth.
Make it a place where students and teachers
search for your knowledge;
Make it a shelter where young people
discover the best of themselves;
Make it a home where all can grow together in wisdom;
And make it a dwelling of light for all
who seek to serve you.

May the teachers be blessed with compassion
and patience;
the staff be filled with joy and peace;
and the students be charged with curiosity and courage
to make this world a home where hope endures.

We ask this in the name of the One
who is wisdom beyond all understanding,
Lord for ever and ever.
Amen.

Blessing of Graduates

Eternal God,
in you we live, and move, and have our being.
In your will we find our purpose,
and in your wisdom we find our joy.

Bless these graduates
who have completed a course of study
and now begin a new part of their lives.

Let them not be troubled about yesterday,
nor anxious about tomorrow,
but let them live fully this day which you have made.

Strengthen their faith in you and in the talents
        you have given them
that they may courageously follow your Spirit
and do your will wherever they go.

When doubt and confusion about their purpose
        surround them,
light their way and give them peace in your plan for them.

When new doors and opportunities open before them,
lead them to make good choices on behalf of those
        most in need.

Let them use the gifts they have received in their studies
that they may become a source of inspiration
and blessing for the world.

And when each day is ended, give them delight in knowing
that the good work you have begun in them
shall come to completion in you.
We ask this through Christ our Lord.
Amen.

Blessing of a Soldier Home from War

Good and gracious God,
we praise you and thank you
for bringing our brother/sister home.
We have missed him/her
and have prayed for his/her safe return,
and you have heard our cry.

Bless him/her now
in this time of homecoming.
Let him/her be embraced by strong and gentle arms,
that he/she may feel again the love of family and friends.
Let him/her see only thanks and pride
in the eyes of those around him/her,
that he/she too may give thanks for the gift of sacrifice.
And let him/her be surrounded by beauty each day,
that he/she may remember the goodness of life.

Heal the wounds that war has inflicted on his/her body
and the scars of violence etched on his/her spirit.
Strengthen any bonds weakened in his/her absence,
and forgive anything that needs to be forgiven.

When memories too painful to bear
        enter his/her thoughts,
may he/she find comfort in the presence of those
        who understand.
And when the faces of the fallen fill his/her dreams,
give him/her the peace only you can bring.

Lord, make us all your instruments of peace,
so that one day we may study war no longer
and live together free from fear
and rejoicing in your kingdom for ever.
We ask this through Christ our Lord.
Amen.

Blessing for Those in Love

Blessed be the God of Love,
for in love all things came to be.
And blessed be those who live in love,
for they who live in love live in God.

Lord, look with favor on your children
who have shared their love with each other
and thus reveal your presence in the world.

Let them rejoice with those who rejoice
and weep with those who weep
so their love may increase
and extend to all they meet.

When darkness diminishes their delight
and time fades their bliss,
guide them with the radiance of your love
that their promise may be steadfast
and their joy complete.

And when they come to the end of their days,
bring them together to live forever
in the love that has no end,
the love of the Father, Son, and Holy Spirit.
Amen.

Blessing of Christmas Cards Before Mailing

God of the universe,
in the beginning, you transformed the dark abyss
into light by speaking your word,
and in the fullness of time, you sent your Son, Jesus,
your Word Made Flesh,
to transform our death into life.
Change, then, the flesh of our lives into words of life,
written upon these Christmas cards we will send.
Take the stories and events of this year,
and make them glimpses of your grace.
Break the walls of separation,
and unite us through the simple gift of a written note.
As we remember the birth of your Son,
bless the words and greetings we will share
and those who will read them
so that the life-giving word you have brought to birth in us
may bring new life to the ends of the earth.
We ask this through Christ our Lord.
Amen.

Blessing of Calendars on the Feast of the Epiphany

In every age, O God, you have been our help.
To the wise men of the East,
your star rose at the appointed time
    to lead them to your Son.
To those at the Jordan, your Spirit descended upon Jesus
to show us that indeed the time of your kingdom
    had come.
And at the wedding banquet of Cana,
time stood still as the guests drank fully
from the bottomless cup of joy that Christ provided.

You created all time and set the stars in motion,
and yet not one second of our life goes by
    without your care.

Bless, then, our timekeepers—
our calendars and clocks, watches and planners,
computers and cell phones, notepads and notebooks.
Help us not be slaves to them
or to fill them so much that we miss your presence
    here and now.

But let us use them to help us be in the right place
        at the right time,
where we can do your will and witness you
        at work in our world.
May we remember each moment and never forget
that you are with us until the end of time.

This we pray in the name of Christ, yesterday and today,
the beginning and the end, Alpha and Omega.
To him be glory and power
through every age for ever and ever.
Amen.

Epiphany Home Blessing

Blessed are you, God of all creation,
for you give us shelter from the cold
and the light of your Word to brighten the night.
We come bearing no gifts,
for everything is a gift from you.
All we can offer is our love for each other
and our faith in your Son.
Transform, then, these humble gifts
into a sign of your presence,
and bless this house and all who come to it.
May this home and this family be a light
for all who are lost and afraid,
a place of peace and hospitality for those in need,
and a sign that you are indeed God with us.
When our long journey has ended,
lead us all by the star of your mercy
that we may come home to you
to the dwelling place you have prepared for us in heaven.
Grant this through Christ our Lord.
Amen.

Lenten Meal Blessing

We bless you, Lord, and we praise you,
for you have given us this meal to share,
provided by the earth and prepared by human hands.
Help us remember those who cannot eat
because of poverty or sickness.
Let the brief hunger we feel this Lent
make us hunger even more for justice.
May this meal strengthen us to do your will.
Blessed be God for ever.
All: *Blessed be God for ever.*

Blessing of Animals

God of all creation,
at the beginning of time
you gave us all the creatures of the earth to be our helpers.
And in your wisdom, these animals,
    like all good things from you,
became more than that. They became our friends.

After our long hours away from home,
in their barks and wagging tails
we see the joy that you, our Creator, must have
when one of your own returns to you.

In our times of sadness and loneliness,
when human relationships become strained and broken,
in their gentle caress and quiet purring
we see the faithfulness that you, our Companion,
offer to all your people.

And when we have become numbed by stress, worry,
    or boredom,
in their natural wonder and untamed majesty
we see the awesome creativity that you, our Maker,
inspire in us that we may revel in the mystery of life.

We ask you, then, to bless these, our animal friends,
that they may have a long and joyful life.
Keep them safe when we cannot be with them,
protect them from sickness and harm,
and heal their wounds.
When the end of their life comes,
grant them a peaceful death free of pain and suffering.
And bless us too, their human companions,
    with your Holy Spirit
that we may care for them well
and be wise and gentle stewards of all your creatures.

We ask this in the name of your Son, Jesus,
who is Lord of all, for ever and ever.
Amen.

Saying Goodbye to a Dying Pet

In the name of God the Father,
who created you and all the animals,
in the name of Jesus the Son,
who spoke of you in parables and stories,
in the name of the Holy Spirit,
in whom all creatures live, move, and have their being,
go now in peace, dear friend.

May you find rest near refreshing waters,
may you lie in cool, green pastures,
and may you warm yourself under the sun that never sets.

You have been my constant companion,
my shadow and confidante,
my comfort and playmate.
You filled my days with life
and brought me endless joy.
For this I give thanks to God
who gave you to me.

Now return to your Maker
who eagerly waits for you
as you waited for me at the end of each day.

In the Father's arms,
let there be no more pain.
Let there be no more suffering.
Let there be only light
as it was on the day God created you.

For our help is in the name of the Lord,
who made heaven and earth.
Blessed be the name of the Lord,
now and for ever.
Amen.

Blessing for All Creation

God of all creation, each morning you send the sun
from the East to bring a new day to birth;
you call the gentle South wind to cool our days
and refresh our lives;
each night the sun sets in the West to bring us the gift
of rest and renewal;
and you summon the great North wind to clothe
the mountaintops in snow and shining splendor.
Send your Holy Spirit over this sacred land we call home,
that the earth may be radiant with your glory
through the care of your people.
From East to West and North to South,
may your blessing be upon every living thing
you have created.
We ask this through Christ, our Lord.
Amen.

This work was typeset in Minion Pro on Apple Macintosh.

Design by Ann Blattner features the art from the apse of the
original church at Saint John's Abbey in Collegeville, Minnesota.